Ballads Of MITHYA

Unfolding the Myths of Womanhood

Dr Smita Kamat Ghosh

Made with ❤ on the BookLeaf Publishing Platform
www.bookleafpub.in
www.bookleafpub.com

Dedication

To the voices lost in history,
To the whispers drowned in silence,
To the dreams caged by myths,
And to the ones who dared to break free.
May these verses serve as echoes of resilience,
As songs of untold truths,
As a hymn for those who rewrite their stories,
And as a tribute to every soul who refuses to be defined
by illusion.
This book is for you.

With courage and conviction,
Dr. Smita Kamat Ghosh

Preface

Myths are not just stories; they are echoes of time, whispered from one generation to the next, shaping identities, expectations, and destinies. Some myths inspire, some control, and some—woven so deeply into the fabric of our existence—become indistinguishable from reality. *Ballads of Mithya* is an ode to these myths, a poetic unraveling of the illusions that have defined womanhood for centuries.

As I wrote *Decoding Mithya*, I found that beyond facts and arguments, there lay emotions—unspoken, raw, and pulsating with truth. Poetry became the voice of these emotions, the space where the silent battles of identity, freedom, and defiance found rhythm. This collection is not just about breaking myths; it is about reclaiming narratives, reimagining femininity, and rediscovering strength in vulnerability.

Each poem in this book is a thread in the larger tapestry of our collective experience. They speak of colors that were never meant to confine, of toys that shaped destinies, of feminism misunderstood, of menstruation silenced, and of financial independence still out of reach for many. These verses are for every woman who has questioned, for every man who has listened, and for every mind willing to unlearn.

Let this book be an exploration, a rebellion, and above all, a tribute—to those who have shattered illusions and those still finding their voice.

Dr. Smita Kamat Ghosh
(Author of Decoding Mithya, Safe Teen Steps, and Mind Aid Pitara)

Acknowledgements

A book, much like a journey, is never walked alone. *Ballads of Mithya* is the culmination of countless conversations, experiences, and silent moments of reflection, all of which have shaped these verses.

I extend my deepest gratitude to the many women and men whose stories have inspired this collection—those who have dared to question, to challenge, and to redefine what it means to exist beyond societal myths. Your voices, struggles, and triumphs breathe life into these poems.

To my family, your unwavering support and belief in my words have been my strength. Thank you for standing by me as I explore the unspoken and unravel the unseen.

To my mentors, colleagues, and fellow thinkers, your insights and encouragement have enriched my understanding of the themes I write about. Our discussions on gender, identity, and empowerment continue to push me to think deeper and write bolder.

To my readers, you are the heart of this book. Whether you find solace, validation, or a spark of rebellion within these pages, know that these words were written for you.

And finally, to poetry itself—the language of the soul. In its rhythm, I have found a way to express the unexpressed, to weave truth into verse, and to give voice to the silent echoes of Mithya.

With gratitude and hope,
Dr. Smita Kamat Ghosh

1. Decoding MITHYA

They wrapped me in colors, pink and blue,
Tied my fate to myths untrue.
Dolls for me, trucks for him,
A silent script, a world grown dim.

They told me grace, not grit, should be mine,
To shrink, to smile, to toe the line.
But within me stirred a voice unsaid,
A fire untamed, a truth unread.

Mithya was woven in cradle songs,
A lullaby of rights and wrongs.
Yet peeling back the layers deep,
I found the self they tried to keep.

Not pink, not blue, not weak, not strong,
Not half a story, not wholly wrong.
I write anew, I break the mold,
A truth reborn, a tale retold.

2. Behind the Pink Veil

They wrapped me in pink before I could choose,
A color so bright yet meant to confuse.
Soft and sweet, tender and mild,
A shade assigned to a quiet child.

Pink for girls, blue for boys,
A myth disguised in ribbons and toys.
But was it always, was it true?
Or just a hue they forced me into?

Once a color bold and free,
Now a chain they tied to me.
Yet beneath the veil, I start to see,
Pink is not my destiny.

Not a label, not a fate,
Not a box to decorate.
I wear my hues, I choose my shade,
A voice unbound, no more afraid.

3. Toy Stories of Silent Conditioning

A doll for me, a truck for him,
Tiny hands shaped by a silent whim.
Tea sets, kitchens, ribbons, and bows,
While he builds towers and cars that glow.

Girls must nurture, boys must lead,
A lesson whispered through plastic and beads.
Wrapped in colors, packed in roles,
Molding futures, shaping souls.

But toys are tools, not chains, not fate,
Not a script to separate.
Let hands explore, let minds be free,
A world unboxed who will we be?

4. The Silent War Within

They taught me grace, they feared my roar,
Told me to bend, to ask for more.
Feminine, they whispered soft, confined,
Yet within me, a fire designed.

She must nurture, she must wait,
She must love but not debate.
Yet when she speaks, when she dares,
They call her harsh unfit to bear.

Feminine, they said, is gentle and small,
Feminism, they warned, will break and brawl.
But what if strength is soft and kind?
What if power loves and binds?

Not a war, not a fight,
Not wrong, not right.
A truth beyond what they divide,
A woman whole, untamed inside.

5. Breaking the Red Silence

They hushed my pain, they hid my stains,
Wrapped my shame in whispered names.
A cycle cursed, yet life it gave,
A burden placed, yet none to save.

Menstruation unspoken, a shadowed tale,
Behind closed doors, behind a veil.
Impure, they said, step aside,
Yet from this blood, all life abides.

Then time moves on, the red runs dry,
A shift, a pause, a silent sigh.
Menopause, they call it the end, they say,
Yet in this change, a new sun ray.

Not cursed, not weak, not past my prime,
A body wise, a soul in time.
From first blood to the final flame,
I stand unbroken, I own my name.

6. Navigating the Maze of Money Myths

They placed a coin in his small hand,
Told him to earn, to own, to stand.
While mine was empty, taught instead,
To stretch, to save, to ask, to beg.

Money a man game, they claim,
A woman touches? Too soft, too tame.
She spends, he plans so myths decree,
A cycle spun in history.

But wealth is wisdom, not just might,
Not gendered rules, not black or white.
Not a privilege, not a fate,
But power held when minds equate.

No pink tax, no silent chains,
No fear of bills, no bound remains.
From purse to plan, from need to dream,
She counts, she earns, she shapes the stream.

7. Hope: The Road Ahead

The road is long, the night is deep,
Echoes of myths, in silence creep.
Yet in the hush, a whisper grows,
A voice once buried, now it flows.

They told us pink was soft and weak,
That strength was loud, not mild or meek.
They wrapped our dreams in ribbons tight,
Yet hope still glowed, a quiet light.

They gave us dolls, they gave us rules,
A world divided into tools.
Yet hands that build and minds that see,
Refuse the chains of history.

They feared our blood, they veiled our pain,
Called it shame, wove guilt in vain.
Yet rivers rage, and oceans swell,
No tide can hush the truth we tell.

Money speaks, they said with ease,
Yet left us out, left us appeased.
But ink on ledgers, coins in hand,
Are ours to hold, to take a stand.

Mithya fades, its shadow thins,
Truth emerges; light begins.
Not just for one, not just for few,
But all who dare to dream anew.

So, step ahead, the path is wide,
With hope and fire side by side.
For myths may break, and walls may fall,
But courage rises—above them all.

8. What's in a Name?

What's in a name, they calmly say,
But here, it's a burden women pay.
Twenty years of a name she's known,
Then comes marriage, and it's overthrown.

A shiny new title, a borrowed tag,
Identity folded like an old, worn rag.
If love falters, or paths unwind,
Her name's the first to be left behind.

Why this weight on her soul's decree,
To bear the cost of society's plea?
A man walks steady, his name intact,
While hers bends, breaks, and retracts.

Her name's her anchor, her battle, her voice,
Let it remain—her unshaken choice.
For what's in a name? The world will see:
It's her essence, her story, her eternity.

9. The Circle Unfolds

It began on a day when the sun hung low,
And the world whispered promises in my ear.
The air, heavy with an unspoken weight,
Carried a rhythm I couldn't yet hear.

Years stretched like rivers winding,
Through valleys of light and shadows deep.
Each turn a story, each moment a thread,
Woven together in the fabric of me.

And now, here I stand,
On the edge of that circle's close.
The same sun rises, its light unyielding,
The same wind carries whispers it chose.

Was it irony, or was it grace?
That the path should loop, not stray.
The beginning and the end entwined,
Marking not loss, but a new way.

The *Bhagavad Gita* breathes within me,
Its voice soft as a mother's hum.
"There is reason in the chaos," it says,
"There is purpose, though it seems undone."

So, I look to the open sky, vast and free,
A horizon unbroken, a breath unbound.
For every ending feeds the soil of growth,
And in each loss, a new self is found.

I carry the circle, but it no longer holds me,
Its weight is a whisper, its shape set free.
The open sky calls, its embrace wide and still,
I step forward now—heart, mind, and will.

10. The Day I Long to Forget

If only time could listen,
And grant me this one plea,
I'd erase the day that marked me,
The day that stole a piece of me.

A day dressed in illusions,
Wrapped in rituals and veiled smiles,
Its weight too heavy for my soul,
Its joy a façade that stretched for miles.

The air was thick with silent screams,
The kind no one dared to hear.
My heart, a prisoner in its own cage,
Bound by love that wasn't clear.

I walked a path not meant for me,
A stranger to my own desires.
Each step a farewell to freedom,
Each promise stoked reluctant fires.

If I could, I'd tear that page,
And watch its ashes drift away.
Let the universe reclaim its sorrow,
Let the winds steal that fateful day.

There's no wisdom I seek from it,
No lesson etched in pain.
Only the wish to unlive that moment,
To never feel its weight again.

Let it be gone, let it dissolve,
Lost to time's unyielding tide.
For in its absence, I might find,
The me that day left behind.

11. Mithya's Veil

In temples, we revere her might, Ma Durga's form,
supreme, alight.
Yet in the world beyond the shrine, Women face a
different line.

Judged by color, deemed less fair, Bias taints the gifts we
share.
Toys that teach a narrowed scope, Clipping wings of
future hope.

Labeled weak, considered frail, Told their efforts often
pale.
Deemed impure in monthly flow, ancient myths that still
bestow.

Denied the reins of finance' art, Trust withheld, a biased
chart.
While goddesses adorn our walls, Living counterparts
face stalls.

Mithya's veil obscures the truth, Contradictions from our youth.
To honor her, both stone and flesh, we must let old judgments thresh.

See the goddess in each face, Granting every woman grace.
Break the chains, dissolve the lies, let equality arise.

12. Breaking the Chains: A Menstrual Awakening

In shadows cast by ancient creeds,
A natural cycle still misreads.
Progress claims a forward stride,
Yet taboos force a girl to hide.

In many homes, she's set apart,
As if her body's sacred art Is something dark, to be
concealed,
A stigma never to be healed.
Are we as free as we profess, when myths of old still
dispossess?

True advancement must ignite
A change in such enduring blight.
Embrace the truth, dispel the fears,
Honor the flow that's marked by years.

For in the blood that women shed,
Lies the power of life widespread.

Let's break these chains, uplift the mind, Leave outdated views behind.
Progress shines when we reveal - The strength in what we once concealed.

13. Nothing is Forever

A new journey, a new way,
A new life begins today.
A new name, a new face,
Moving forward, finding place.

"न जायते म्रियते वा कदाचि-
न्नायं भूत्वा भविता वा न भूयः।
अजो नित्यः शाश्वतोऽयं पुराणो
न हन्यते हन्यमाने शरीरे॥"
(Bhagavad Gita 2.20)

As the Gita gently sings,
Nothing lasts, not even strings.
Some hands we hold, then let go,
Some hearts drift, like rivers flow.

Not all ties are meant to stay,
Some fade; some walk away.

But love remains, in silent air,
A memory, always there.

14. Decoding Mithya Through the Bhagavad Gita

Illusions woven, myths untold,
Stories crafted; centuries old.
Bound by whispers, shaped by fear,
Yet truth remains, always nearby.

"असतो मा सद्गमय।
तमसो मा ज्योतिर्गमय।
मृत्योर्मा अमृतं गमय॥"

(Brihadaranyaka Upanishad 1.3.28, echoed in the Gita's wisdom)

From falsehood, lead me to truth,
From darkness, into light's youth.
From the fleeting, to the eternal way,
Breaking chains that bid us stay.

Pink is not weak, nor toys define,
Womanhood thrives beyond a line.
Freedom lies not in gold or fame,

But in knowing, we are not the same.

"न कर्मणामनारम्भान्नैष्कर्म्यं पुरुषोऽश्नुते।"
(Bhagavad Gita 3.4)

Action births wisdom, step by step,
Not in silence, nor regret.
Break the myths, unmask the lies,
For within you, the truth resides.

Mithya fades, as dawn draws near,
Through the Gita's voice—strong and clear.

15. Unchained by Color: A Bhagavad Gita Reflection

Bhagavad Gita – Chapter 2, Verse 14
"Mātrā-sparśās tu kaunteya, śhītoṣhṇa-sukha-duḥkha-dāḥ
Āgamāpāyino 'nityās, tāṁs titikṣhasva bhārata"

Like seasons shift from cold to warm,
Like waves retreat, then rise in form,
Joy and sorrow, fleeting tide,
Endure them all, let none decide.

They wrapped me in pink, so soft, so bright,
A color of calm, of delicate light.
Yet, who decreed this shade for me?
Is not my soul vast and free?

The sky at dusk wears crimson hue,
The ocean deep is painted blue.
A flower blooms in hues untold,
Why must I fit in pink's stronghold?

The Gita whispers, firm yet kind,
No fleeting touch can chain the mind.
No color holds the soul confined,
For truth is vast—unshaped, unlined.

Pink is passing, so is blue,
Mere shades that shift in worldly view.
Yet I remain, untouched, untied,
In dharma's light, my spirit wide.

So break the myth, let colors blend,
No hue defines, no shade can end.
For in the vastness of the sky,
The soul is free—it dares to fly.

16. Breaking the Chains, Rising Again

Bhagavad Gita – Chapter 18, Verse 63
"Vimṛśyaitad aśeṣeṇa, yathecchasi tathā kuru"
**"Reflect deeply upon this wisdom, then act as you deem
fit."**

They said I was fragile, they said I was weak,
A whisper in winds, too timid to speak.
Bound by myths, in silence confined,
A tale unwritten, a fate assigned.

They gave me colors, they gave me roles,
They stitched their rules into my soul.
"Stay within, don't dream too wide,
The world is vast, but not your ride."

Yet deep within, a fire grew,
A silent storm, a force so true.
For truth is strong, it does not wane,
Like rivers cut through rock and pain.

The Gita speaks in wisdom deep,
A call to rise, to wake from sleep.
No chain is real, no fate is sealed,
The mind is vast—its wounds are healed.

I rise again, like dawn so bold,
Not bound by myths, not bought or sold.
I shape my path, I break the mold,
A tale untold—a truth retold.

So let them whisper, let them say,
That storms should bend, that fire should stay.
Yet here I stand, in light, in grace,
Unbound, unchained—I take my place.

17. Rise Like the Phoenix, Rooted in Strength

Bhagavad Gita – Chapter 2, Verse 47
"Karmanye vadhikaraste, ma phaleshu kadachana"
"You have the right to perform your duty, but never to the fruits of your actions."

The flames once raged, they tried to consume,
The weight of myths, a world in gloom.
Yet from the ashes, bright and strong,
The phoenix sings its battle song.

They called her weak, they called her frail,
A bird too small, too soft, too pale.
Yet fire within refused to die,
She spread her wings and kissed the sky.

But flight alone will not suffice,
A land must bloom, a world precise.
The soil must change, deep and true,
A place where strength and hope renew.

No chains of color, no voice restrained,
No myths of "less," no dreams contained.
For roots run deep when truth is sown,
Where courage thrives, the soul has grown.

So break the mold, unbind the past,
Build the ground where dreams hold fast.
A girl must rise, not just alone,
But in a world where she is known.

Like the phoenix, she will ascend,
Not just to fly, but to transcend.
For not just wings, but roots run deep,
A world reborn, a promise to keep.

18. Unchained Wings

*"Purusham prakriti-stham cha, viddhyubhau prakriti-jau
gunan".*
(Bhagavad Gita 13:22)
*"Both man and nature are bound by qualities, yet
wisdom frees the soul."*

"Boys don't cry," they always say,
"Be strong, be tough, don't walk away."
Yet, does the river not carve the stone?
Does the sky not weep when storms are blown?

They cage his heart in iron walls,
Hide his wounds, ignore his calls.
But strength is not in fists held tight,
It's in the courage to stand for right.

Let him feel, let him be,
Not just armor—wild and free.
Break the myth, unchain the past,

A boy is more than a mold cast.

19. Breaking the Myth, Embracing the Truth

Bhagavad Gita – Chapter 4, Verse 7
"Yada yada hi dharmasya, glanir bhavati bharata,
Abhyutthanam adharmasya, tadatmanam srjamy aham."
"Whenever righteousness declines and injustice rises, I
manifest to restore balance."

They wrote the rules, they drew the lines,
Bound us all in their design.
"Girls are soft, boys are strong,
Stay in place, don't prove them wrong."

Pink for her, blue for him,
A silent script, a tale so grim.
Toys, careers, and ways to feel,
Defined before we learned what's real.

Yet truth is light—it breaks the night,
Shatters myths with burning might.
A girl can lead, a boy can cry,

Dreams have wings that touch the sky.

Not in colors, not in roles,
But in hearts and fearless souls.
Rise, unlearn, reclaim, renew,
The world belongs to all—not just a few.

www.ingramcontent.com/pod-product-compliance
Lightning Source LLC
LaVergne TN
LVHW010926200726
843509LV00013B/2097